Inner Peace
an Obtainable Goal

Vivian Stevenson

First Edition

LCCN: 2013900373

ISBN: 9780615749181

Visit www.vivianstevenson.com

CONTENTS

Acknowledgement

As a reader, I noticed that Authors thanked lots of people at the beginning of their books.

I now know why; to undertake the writing of a book requires the help and support of many. It is truly a joint venture. And so, I would like to thank my family and friends and yes my life's experiences that have gone into the making of this book.

A special thanks goes out to Lisa and Gary McSherry for sharing their river home as a quite place to write; to Jenny Haynes for guidance and editing assistance; to Stephen Wilton for helping me with design, marketing and advertising; and to Kathy Tashner and Jackie Durnett for always being there, and believing in me even when I didn't.

INTRODUCTION

I hope to show how with diligence, practice and knowledge you can acquire and ***maintain*** a peaceful life.

Peace does not mean to be in a place where there is no noise, trouble or hard work; it simply means to be in the midst of those things and still be calm and peaceful. While working on the book, I had many challenges; the last one was being laid off from my job. Using the principals of the book I have weathered the storm's and can personally attest to the fact the principals outlined in the book do work.

Peace is our natural state of being, and so when we are "in it", peace is taken for granted. It is only when we have gotten off course that we become aware of the loss, think about and long for it.

My desire is that this book will help you become aware of why and when you start to slip away from your natural state of peace, thereby eliminating a lot of potential Hell.

Have you ever noticed that when we are "O.K." with ourselves, with our life, the world is a better place? Now the world has not changed one iota, but through our eyes it looks

new, beautiful, and full of hope and promise.

Here's to bright and beautiful tomorrows.

Chapter One

THE HEART'S DESIRE

We've all heard the expression: "You don't know what you've got till it's gone", and so it is with peace. When we are at peace, all seems right in our world, and we don't give it a second thought. We seldom, if ever think: "Thank Goodness for this time"! However, let our world turn upside down, and see how readily the "woe is me" comes to mind. Why is this? Because peace is our natural state of being, it's like being healthy. Few of us wake up each morning and are thankful for our well being, unless we have been ill or know someone who is. The good news is that with peace being our true nature, all we need to experience it is to acknowledge that the ultimate power to change lies within each of us.

The first step is being aware and wanting to change. This sounds simple, but most people do not believe they can change, or even if they have the desire and belief, do not know how. Because of this, often times they subconsciously sabotage themselves.

How many times have you thought: "it's always been

like this", and then a sense of despair sets in? Sometimes these thoughts go back for generations, or they may even be a part of our society. It seems like an insurmountable task to break free. After all, it's always been like this, how can "I" break this cycle? The first step is wanting to, and obviously you do or you would not be reading this book. Bill Murray, in the movie "Groundhog Day" woke each day to the same day over and over. Finally, tired of the repetition of his life, he started doing things differently. Small changes at a time to achieve different results; at the end of the movie, his internal changes had brought about a new day for him. I said it was because he wanted a new life, a male friend of mine said it was to get the girl. Whatever his motivation it worked.

If you scanned the index of this book, you might have noticed one of the longest chapters in the book is this one on desire! The reason for this is that desire is the biggest part of bringing about any change.

Do you know your compelling reason for wanting to change? Do you know what you hope to accomplish? How will you feel? What will your life look like? What is the motivation behind your desire to change? Whatever your motivation is stick to it and you will see results.

Pause a moment in your reading and take the time to do the following exercise:

Exercise:

- **Do you know your compelling reason for wanting to change?**

Do you know you know what you hope to accomplish?

- **How will you feel?**

- **What will your life look like?**

While wanting to achieve peace is the first step, there is obviously a need for action. Anyone who knows me knows that I am a goal-action oriented person, but when it's your problem, the call to action is not always clear. How many times have I said: "if only I knew what to do, I'd be happy to do it". How many times have I thought: "where and how do I start? What should I do?"

These very questions came up time and again in the various stages of writing this book. My fears of "how to" and "could I" surfaced more times than I want to admit. They paralyzed me into wanting to read a book, rather than write one.

"The people in the world that are crazy enough to think that they can change the world are the ones that do. "

Apple Computers, Inc.

"As any change must begin somewhere, it is the single individual who will experience it and carry it through. The change must indeed begin with an individual; it might be any one of us. Nobody can afford to look round and to wait for somebody else to do what he is loath to do himself."

Carl G. Jung

It is important to remember that these questions without action can keep you grounded in the past. Early in my sales career, I was told: "Do something, even if it is wrong, at least you will be learning what does not work." If you do nothing, there can be no change.

The change needs to take place on many levels. The physical, the mental and the emotional, all must be addressed at some point. How this is done is as individual as each of us. Some prefer to work through things from the mental and some from the feeling side of our nature. Either way, we all must face the emotional changes that need to take place when we challenge ourselves. Whichever way suits is great; taking some positive deliberate action is key. Just do it. When I use the logical side, it's with pen and paper, writing out my thoughts and feelings. If you choose this method be O.K. with just allowing anything and everything to flow out; be open, do not judge what you find yourself writing, just keep going until there is nothing left to write, and then try to write some more. Sometimes, I write out what I think the worst case scenario might be and face the fear associated with it. The beauty of this is that there is no right or wrong; any insight that you might get is a valuable piece of the puzzle. If you choose this method, be sure that your thoughts can be kept in a safe place. After all, this is your personal journey, and speaking from experience I can say if you think it might be read you will censor your thoughts and feelings thus diminishing the results.

Sometimes I try the feeling approach, listening to my heart, asking what is the loving thing to do, how would I want to be treated? The Golden Rule: "Do unto others as you will have them do unto you" is always a good way to approach a situation, and it is a simple and easy rule to follow. We all know how we want to be treated, or by contrast how we would feel if someone did something to us, so just turn it around when questioning your actions.

Take for instance my concerns of being controlled. The physical aspect was that I found myself in circumstances where people controlled my actions. My emotional reaction to this was to be angry or to shut down, to withdraw. Emotionally I felt I was the victim. In order to heal from this it was necessary for me to look at each part of the equation.

Physically ...why was I in this situation? What could I do to change it? Was it possible to remove myself?

Mentally ...the first question I had to ask was, were the others really trying to control me or did I perceive it that way because I had such an issue with control? A lot of the time it was my projection of the issue. The restricting binds had been placed on me by me and my beliefs. However, there are times they were brought about by others. Then I had to decide what and how I wanted to change. Did I need to change my thoughts; my boundaries; my relationships? When making changes remember the important thing is to do something. Fear has a way of rooting us even if we do not like where we are.

Emotionally ...with the belief that others controlled me, I felt I had no rights, no voice in my life. I was a victim. To heal it was necessary to take responsibility for myself, for my life and to become empowered by these actions. It is important to remember any core issue, as control was for me, should be taken one step at a time.

And yes there was much turmoil and pain. But there

15

was turmoil and pain where I was, and having made the changes I am now in a much better space and I am glad I stayed the course. Let me say here before I go further, this book is not designed to take the place of personal counseling and in the case of some behaviors your best course of action is to seek outside help. Each case is separate and distinct, and only you know what is best.

Pause a moment in your reading and take the time to do the following exercise:

Express Your Stress:

- **Think of an issue that is bothering you, something that has been causing you some stress.**

- **Write what you are upset about, how you feel about what has happened.**

- **Write your feelings not only about the issue but the people involved.**

- **Then write what you wish had happened instead.**

- **The person at fault could be you; there are times that I know that I did not handle a situation well and wish that I could have the opportunity for a "do over".**

The ego does not let up once a course of action has been taken; it will keep you wondering if you've made the right decision. My benchmark for knowing if I've arrived at the best solution is found by listening to my gut; for that feeling in the pit of your stomach that lets you know when things are right or not. This is where your subconscious can bypass the emotional traps of your heart and head.

Depending on the topic, sometimes there is no good feeling to be had other than knowing you have done the very best you can. Some decisions in life are painful, but the knowledge that change needed to take place gives you the strength and courage to see these difficult times through to the end.

Be sure to acknowledge your success, each step, regardless of how big or small it is. This allows you to see the positive growth that you are accomplishing. Your ego will tell you not to make a big deal out of it, but it is a big deal. Each time you bring to your conscious mind the evidence that you are making progress you are building the concept of the new you, your new foundation to build upon. Do not be discouraged if you are not perfect the first time. The key is to keep trying, because with each effort you are putting into place the new patterns, the healthier patterns that will allow you a happier, healthier life. No one said it was easy, but it is worth it. After all, what in life does not require training to perfect the skill? This is no different. So when that little voice in your head starts with the negative self-talk shut it out, take action that will reinforce the positive side of you and be gentle with yourself, after all it takes about 30 days before something becomes a new habit.

The Golden Rule is always a good way to approach a situation.

The closest to perfection a person ever comes is when he fills out a job application form.

Evan Escar

The part played by the unconscious in all our acts is immense, and that played by reason very small. The unconscious acts like a force still unknown.

Gustave Le Bon

By understanding the unconscious we free ourselves from its domination.

Carl G. Jung

Pause a moment in your reading and take the time to do the following exercise:

Exercise: Acknowledge Your Accomplishments

- **Think back over your past accomplishments.**

- **Jot them down, acknowledging to yourself that you have made positive changes in your life; that you are more than capable of doing so again.**

- **Keep this list handy and update it as you begin to claim even more of what you accomplish.**

Just as we resist change, so will people around us. You will find that as you start making changes in your life, others may not like this, and they might do "things" to bring you back into your old ways, for no other reason than change is fearful to everyone. They might dislike the condition or situation as much as you but are scared to take the steps to change. The current problem is known, but what change may bring is not, and how you and the people around you will be affected is not. Be prepared for things like teasing, ridicule and other forms of manipulation that might be used to bring you back to the old self. Recognize this for what it is, your growth, and your change, and stay the course of healing. There was a time, if you said anything about my home, I would have been upset, even offended, as this was one of my "buttons". Knowing this, my friend said to me: "I have been watching this container in the refrigerator grow mold". This was at the beginning stages of a transformation for me, so I decided to try a different approach and replied, without emotion: "Why have you not just thrown it away? It would have taken less time". This response was completely out of character, and when he did not get the fight that he wanted, I heard him mutter, "Darn book". This type of resistance should be seen as a good sign, a sign that you are making progress.

Another reason that people do not choose to have peace in their life is that they do not want it; they enjoy drama, and the pendulous swings of emotion, the highs and lows that come from living their life without peace. There was a time, when I thought that kind of excitement was what life was all about. We've all heard people say "yeah we fight like heck, but it sure is fun to make up". It is also dished out daily on TV and in many books we read. If you are one of those people, think of what you are doing to yourself and to those you love. What are you teaching to those closest to you? Should you need extra motivation at times to continue on with your quest for peace, remember that as you heal and grow healthier so do those around you! The real joy and excitement in life comes from being balanced, where the Ups and Downs are moderate. We've all seen children get over excited; the enthusiasm/thrill of a situation after a while becomes an agitation and results in unrest. We cannot sustain these larger than life feelings and when they leave us we feel let down. Everyone knows that it is better to eat properly than to rely on a "quick sugar fix", the low of a sugar crash is usually worse than if we had not had the sugar high in the first place. Life is a series of cycles and growth, and no one will dispute that these are stressful times. However, we can make the road a little smoother for ourselves and subsequently for others, where we stay in the state of peace and joy for longer and longer periods of time and avoid the radical emotional swings we have grown accustomed to.

If you are not experiencing joy in your life, make a commitment to yourself now that you will consciously bring it into your life. Do this by daily visualizing the image of your joy, feel it, allow it to become a part of you, engage in those activities that make you joyful more often.

∽

Another reason that people do not choose to have peace in their life is that they do not want to; they enjoy the drama, and the pendulous swings of emotion, the highs and lows that come from living your life without peace.

∽

Pause a moment in your reading and take the time to do the following exercise:

Exercise: Finding your Joy

- What brings you joy? Is it a smile or the laughter of a child? The ability to help another? The Sunrise on the Ocean, a cool mountain breeze, it can be something as fanciful as the image of a pixie dancing among the flowers.

- Jot down as many things as you can think of, make a mental note of how and when you are joyful.

- At the end of each day write down those things that brought you joy during the day. This will accomplish several things, first you can add them to your list and it'll help you realize how often you are allowing joy into your life.

- Make a conscious decision to spend more and more time doing the things which bring you joy. Monitor your efforts by including this in your journal.

- Think of ways you can incorporate them into

your life. Your ego will tell you there isn't enough time, but there is, and you and all those around you will benefit.

We all have roles we play in our relationships. Some of the main unhealthy characters are:

The Victim, the Martyr and the Persecutor.

The **victim** feels as if they have no choice in things and are always at the mercy of those around them. They are held captive by their childhood, education, someone or a situation in their life that they feel they have no control over.

The **martyr** knows there are choices, but feels they must "give over" for the people in their life, but then resents having done so. When we are in this particular cycle of life, we switch back and forth between the two roles, depending on who we are interacting with or how we feel at the moment. But the truth is the victim and the martyr is one and the same. It has taken me a while, but I now believe that if it is not right for me, "it" is not right for the other person involved either. When I start feeling like the victim/martyr, I stop and question my motives. Am I being unreasonable and just throwing a pity party for myself, or am I buying into something that is not really healthy for any of the parties involved? I do not believe in a world where I must suffer so that

27

others can have. This would mean that I have less value than another person, that someone else has more right to happiness, peace and joy than I do. The "Course In Miracles" talks about special relationships, ones that allow and demand special treatment because of how we have defined them. A special relationship is the birthplace of many of the unhealthy roles that we play.

The *persecutor*, the bad one, must be present in order to complete the cycle. They appear to be in control, in charge, but the truth is they are as unhappy as the other two roles. However, it is rare that the victim/martyr sees this until they are on the road to healing the relationship, or the script would not work. Either way, there is no peace; it does not matter which role you are playing. There have been times in my life where I starred in all three roles. A one woman act, I blamed myself (the persecutor) for some perceived fault (the victim) and then justified my actions because I felt I had no other choice (the martyr).

This is a perfect example of how our life's lessons/ issues are all about us. So whether you enlist the aid of another co-star or you decide on a one-person play, it makes no difference. The lesson is still the same, as is the way to work through it. Take the other person out of the picture and ask: "What is my lesson, what can I change to bring about a peaceful resolution?" The peaceful center is where we make healthy decisions, which break the patterns of the past and set us free from the ongoing cycles that plague us.

Pause a moment in your reading and take the time to do the following exercise:

Exercise: Write Out Your Play

- Write out a scenario that keeps recurring in your life.

- Give the cast their roles, who is the victim, the martyr, the persecutor? Try to do this without fault or blame.

- See how each player is dependent on the other playing their role.

- Now rewrite the script to bring about a new alternate ending to your story. Think how YOU can change your role, to help break these unhealthy patterns that are in place.

This exercise is designed to help you see the pattern, thus stopping the ongoing cycle by a mental awareness rather than remaining in the emotional default of continuing the old ways.

The next time you find yourself in turmoil, ask: "Do I want to continue my old patterns, or do I want peace? Which role am I playing and why?" Identifying the role and why you have chosen it will provide you with the very knowledge you need to overcome it. Whether you choose victim or martyr it is usually because you think you have no choice. Sometimes the situations "must be" for the moment but remember that even if the events cannot change on the surface your mental attitude about them can, and from there other changes will be forthcoming. Let's say due to circumstances you become a caregiver. Necessary as it is, it adds to your stress. You can still choose to change your mental attitude and shift your thoughts about it though; thereby changing how you feel. Those fortunate times, when the situation can change if you act upon it, are very powerful times indeed.

The more you apply these principles to your life, the

sooner you'll become aware of when you are slipping from that peaceful center. At that moment, STOP, stop and ask yourself, PEACE or PATTERN, which do I want? When you do, you will have taken the first and very important step in breaking the pattern and moving along the road to becoming a healthier, more peaceful person. As with all things, the more often you do them, the easier they become. The wonderful thing is, that as you do this, all aspects of your life, all relationships in your life will benefit.

Review your day, did you choose to bring joy into your life today?

Did you replay a pattern, if so, which role did you play, and what was the core issue?

If you want a more defined snap shot of what you are experiencing make up your own key to help pinpoint what is going on. Was the issue one of Anger, Control, Judgment, Fear, or Guilt?

If it wasn't Joy-Love what was it? Look past the drama and see the core nature. Were there physical contributing factors, were you tired, hungry, did you have expectations that weren't met? Seeing the patterns will help narrow down the issues. I strongly believe when this is done there will only be 1 or maybe 2 issues, all other things stem from them, this not only shows you what you need to focus on but also just how manageable it really is.

Take for example my friend Martha; Martha knew she had a project to complete by week's end.

She had gathered her data, and knew that all she had to do was "pull it together in the proper format" she had plenty of time. The morning it was due however, her project manager wanted her pulled from the current job to use her expertise on another project; one that Martha really wanted to work on. To accomplish this she had to work through lunch and when a co-worker stopped by and asked her for help she replied angrily "I can't do everything", and stormed away from her desk, leaving her co-worker confused and hurt. Later that day after she had completed her task, Martha remembered her "joy list" and went for a walk outside, and enjoyed the moment. She then found her co-worker and apologized.

In this example Martha played the role of the victim (V) the martyr (M), and the Persecutor (P). Her physical contributing factors were stress (S) and hunger (H). The issue was control or feeling as if she had no control.

So for this day the calendar might look like V/M/P with Triggers of S & H.   The core issue was control (C).   Her

34

joy came from being in nature (J-nature). I would suggest you pick a method to make the core issue and joy stand out over the other keys, this will help you focus and see where you are.

Use a 30 day calendar to help you keep seeing where you are in your growth, what needs to be addressed, your progress and your successes. As you practice the exercises in the book and advance through the month, you'll see your calendar will have more notes of JOY and less of the negative traits that have been in your life.

Peace or Pattern, which do you want?

No arsenal or NO weapon in the arsenals of the world is so formidable as the will and moral courage of free men and women.

Ronald Reagan

Summary of Chapter 1

- What is your motivation behind your desire to change?

- By making these changes what do you hope to accomplish?

- Make notes of your successes/changes. If it helps keep a journal.

- Recognize the roles and patterns you play out. Determine which of these you want to rewrite and how.

- When in turmoil stop and ask yourself Peace or Pattern; make the conscious choice.

- Know in any given circumstance some aspect can always be changed for the good. It might be only your mental outlook but that alone will change your world.

- Think about what brings joy, true joy to you. Is it a smile or the laughter of a child, the ability to help another? The Sunrise on the Ocean, a cool mountain breeze, it can be something as fanciful as the image of a pixie dancing among the flowers.

- If you are not experiencing joy in your life, make a commitment to yourself now that you will consciously bring it into your life. Do this by daily visualizing the image of your joy, feel it, allow it to become a part of you, keep this as a part of your journal.

Chapter Two

FROM WHY, TO HOW

There are those who say that a peaceful existence in today's world is unattainable. There is no doubt that we live in troubled and stressful times. I am not discounting the pain, violence and despair we see in our lives and on television. What I am saying is that we all have choices to make. As the Serenity Prayer says..."grant us the serenity to accept what we cannot change, the courage to change that which we can, and the wisdom to know the difference". In this there is much peace and wisdom.

What I am addressing are the situations in our lives that we can change. Sometimes, all we can change is our "outlook". How we choose to perceive the situation. In this way, even the things that we appear to have no control over, we can control by how we internalize them. In this way we create our reality. As adults, we cannot change the things that happened to us as children, but we can see how even the worst of experiences have made us stronger. After all, there is truth in the expression, "what does not kill us, makes us stronger". The most difficult times in your life shape you. You choose how.

Pause a moment in your reading and take the time to do the following exercise:

Exercise: What made you stronger?

Think back over your life. Now write down some of those things that sprang to mind. Then pick one; think how it has made you stronger, more capable.

We've all had them; acknowledge them for the positive effects that they have had on you.

"Every act of conscious learning requires the willingness to suffer an injury to one's self-esteem. That is why you children, before they are aware of their own self importance learn so easily; and why older persons, especially if vain or important, cannot learn at all."

Thomas S. Szas

"You learn more from getting your butt kicked than from getting it kissed."

Tom Hanks

For example, Chad had a difficult childhood, and was in and out of the foster care system. As the father of three children he consciously provides his children with the love and stability he felt was missing in his early years.

If you see only fear and a lack, then you will manifest this in your life. In the introduction I asked if you had ever noticed that when things are going well, the world seems a better place. By the same token, when things go wrong it feels as if the whole world is against you. This is an example of "what you focus on is what you will bring about". In the movie "Ghostbusters" there is a scene where the group of Ghostbusters is told to think only happy thoughts, because whatever they thought about would come to be. One group member, as a child, had been afraid of the "Stay-Puff Marshmallow Man"; being told not to thinks scary things, he of course did indeed think of what frightened him. There appeared a giant marshmallow man. The others could not believe that anyone would be afraid of the "Stay- Puff Marshmallow Man".

The reality is that all of our fears are like the

43

marshmallow man. If you think about them, you will manifest them, bring them to yourself, and make them real. And, because they are your fears they are real to you. So, just what is it that you wish to believe in, to create? Suppose, you decide that the world is a friendly place, instead of the unfriendly place you have seen before. Suppose you decide that everyone likes you. Suppose that you felt that something good was about to happen. Would these new thoughts make a difference in your daily life? I think that they would.

Pause a moment in your reading and take the time to do the following exercise:

Exercise: What do you believe in?

Do you believe you can bring about positive change in your life?

Be sure to listen to yourself talk, to those random thoughts you think. They will tell you want you really think.

In Scott Peck's book, "The Road Less Traveled", he discusses, early in the book, the idea of each of us having our own view of the world. The first time this concept really rang true to me I was totally miserable, sitting in the middle lane of traffic. I looked at the car on either side, one driver was fussing with their passenger, the other's radio was loudly belting out a song and the driver was singing along. We all had the same external conditions but each of us was experiencing the day differently. As a psychiatrist, Peck says most people have an outdated view or map of the world. We think of ourselves as the way we were, we think that the people in our life have not and will not change, and then we react based on old data. All of life brings about change and with each new experience we choose how we respond. Imagine the injustice that we do to ourselves and others by not acknowledging these changes.

We are responsible for how we respond to others. Are you finding ways to help or overcome the situation, or do you contribute to the problem by your words, action and thoughts? There are times throughout the day where we must make a choice. Do I add to the problem or am I a part of the solution? The other day I received some emails that were in my opinion rude. I chose not to respond right away, deciding I needed some time before reacting. Several times throughout the day when I'd see the e-mail I wanted to respond. Respond with a not so nice e-mail of my own. In the end, I asked myself; what is it for? Why do I want to carry this drama on?" And, I chose to delete the message and the attitude from my day. It simply was not worth the ensuing e-mail battle.

Peace is a topic that our ego fights against. The opening statement usually starts with "yea but"! How many times when trying to control, convince, or cajole someone to your way of thinking have you used those very words? This should be a red flag. Other phrases that alert you to an ego attack are; "it's not fair; if only; I cannot do anything about it; why me"?

"Why" is one of those words that will drive you crazy, whether it is a three year old or thirty year old asking. The why question does not get any better with age; it will still put us in a downward spiral. It is the ego's way of keeping us from dealing with the real problem.

Trying to determine someone else's motivations is impossible. They usually are unaware of WHY they do what they do! So how could they explain it to you? Even more ludicrous, is trying to get inside their heads and figure it out yourself.

Another reason not to ask why is that it keeps you in the victim/martyr role, that place where you are at the whim of outside forces....a place where your peace is constantly threatened.

Usually when you ask why, there are two motivations to the question, one to find fault and the other is to understand. Asking someone else why puts them on the defensive. It forces the person responding to justify their actions and the response it invokes is usually defensive.

The question to ask is HOW?

How can I change this; how can I express my needs and myself differently?

BREAK THE PATTERN!! One way might be by asking, "Can you help me understand ...; or will you walk me through how you came to this decision/choice on this." If you are sincere it will come through, and hopefully bring about a different response.

Pause a moment in your reading and take the time to do the following exercise:

Exercise: Rename that button HOW

I'd recommend thinking of one of your buttons that's been pushed over and over again. Think of your favorite or least favorite depending how you look at it. You know, the way so and so bothers you when you say, or do....those annoying traits that cause the same reaction/fight each and every time. You have it in your mind already, and can probably think of several. Go with the one that came to mind first.

The next time this comes up, ask yourself:

"How can I express myself"?

"How can I respond to get a different outcome?"

"How can I break this pattern?"

"What about this really bothers me?"

"How can I express what I need in a way to bring about a positive change"?

Perhaps the answer is to say to the person before it comes up again, "Hey, I know that you don't mean to, but when this happens I feel…, then express yourself in a kind and loving way. Be prepared to hear their side, and don't forget the "Golden Rule" when interacting with people.

Write out and think through these exercises, this way you will be ready the next time your button is activated. You will be able to respond in a different way, which will bring about a new result more in keeping with a healthier resolution to your problem, and a healthier you.

Remember, peace does not come from how they respond to you, but how you respond to them and from your knowledge that you have taken a very valuable step forward. This is another empowering step toward your goal of inner peace.

A true leader has the confidence to stand alone, the courage to make tough decisions and the compassion to listen to the needs of others. He does not set out to be a leader, but becomes one by the equality of his actions, and the integrity of his intent.

General Douglas McArthur

Summary of Chapter 2

- Describe a difficult time in your life. Now describe how it has made you a stronger, more capable person.

- Become aware of your self talk, as these conversations tell you what you really believe. Which ones do you need to rewrite, think them through, have the rewrite in place so the next time your old negative talk starts you can stop it. Bring yourself back to the new and improved script, thus reprogramming your thinking.

- Think of a recurring issue, one of your "hot buttons" and ask yourself:

- "How can I express myself differently"?

- "How can I respond to get a different outcome?"

- "How can I break this pattern"?

- "What about this really bothers me"?

- "How can I express what I need in a way that brings about a positive change"?

- "Why" is the Ego's way of keeping us from moving forward, it enforces the belief in the victim and martyr roles, and it puts people on the defensive.

- Do your actions add to the problem or are you a part of the solution?

Chapter Three

RELEASE THE JUDGEMENT

We are taught from a very young age to judge. Judge whether something is right or wrong, safe or dangerous. Some judgment is not only healthy, it's necessary to our survival. However, the judgment I am referring to is the judgment that robs us of our peace. You know the kind; it's judgmental, critical, and mean spirited. It has a bite to it. It's the kind that makes you feel as if there were two people sitting on either side of your head, each whispering something, both vying for your attention, the type of judgment that renders doubt and confusion, rather than peace and direction.

Writing this book, I came face to face with my own doubts and fears, those little voices whispering, sometimes shouting, feelings of inadequacy. In moments of weakness I judged myself incapable of completing the task. This book has been a wonderful means to help me redefine fear. I now think of fear as the fuel to success. Fear is not the villain, but rather the guide, or motivation to what needs to be changed, and the greater your fear, the greater your need to change. You can choose to allow fear and doubts to be the catalyst for failure or success. Henry Ford once said, "Whether you believe you can do a thing or not, you are right". Which do you choose? Do not be fooled into thinking that there is a middle ground here, for there is not. To make no decision is a decision. To do nothing means that you have chosen to postpone your growth and are allowing fear to immobilize you.

Remember the little red engine, who said "I think I can, I think I can." The reality is if you think you can, you can. But you must be courageous enough to try and stay the course when fear, doubt and resistance to change come along.

Fear is like a heat seeking missile. You can't outrun it, hide from it, duck it..But if you walk right at it, it misses you completely. It goes right pass you, as if you were just an illusion.

mwarrior.com

I must, in all candor, say that I do not think myself fit for the Presidency.

Abraham Lincoln

I was once asked to write about an emotion. After much thought, it occurred to me that the emotion that caused me the most difficulty was Doubt. I would like to share those thoughts with you.

⏤⏤⏤

"Seeds of Doubt-A Conversation with Self"

Hey, how's it going?

Where have you been?

What's this, you say you don't recognize me?

Sure you do.

My name is Doubt, I was born in the 13th month, under the astrological sign of Confusion and I am closely linked to despair, and if left unchecked, even depression.

I run with some heavy hitters I know, but I am up to it. You see, it's all in the subtle way that I handle things. Never hit them over the head when the quiet, slow approach works, I always say. And it does too. By the time I get through with you, you won't know which end is up. Heck, sometimes I

58

am so good, you're not even certain if you know the right thing to focus on. You can find yourself thinking maybe that wasn't even the real issue, maybe I should...

Do you recognize me now?

Sure you do.

We used to see a lot more of each other. Then you started all that "going within" stuff, getting your answers from some higher voice. Listening with your heart and gut; not your head. Well, I just wanted to ask...are you sure that it's a higher voice you're hearing, or is it just your imagination?

After all, that gut could be the bean burrito you ate for lunch. Just thought I'd ask.

Be seeing you around.

Doubt is an emotion that gives a lot of us trouble.

Over the years I have come up with some helpful tips to use when I doubt myself.

The first is "When in doubt, don't", it is rare that a

decision has to be made in the spur of the moment. I find, most of the time, you do have time to wait and think things through. It's the ego that wants to make a snap decision, and most of the time these decisions are of course based on past behavior/patterns. Take for example the e-mail I received, by not responding right away, I was able to put enough time/ distance between the rudeness of the e-mail and myself and was able to detach from the drama. And it did feel good, and I did acknowledge my success, each time doing so becoming easier and easier.

Another tip concerning doubt is that perhaps the reason you are having difficulty is because as of yet you haven't all the information you need to make a decision. Step back and see if this is so, then set about getting the information or simply wait and give it time to progress. Time is a wonderful thing when working with the emotion of doubt.

My final tip on doubt is: If you have come to the point where you do need to have a decision, you have as much information as you can get and you are still bothered as to what to do, listen to the answer in your gut. As stated earlier, we process information in our head, (mentally) our heart, (emotionally) and in our gut (a place of natural knowing). If you are fighting this, think back over the times when you went against that little voice in your gut and wished you hadn't. At least try it!

Pause a moment in your reading and take the time to do the following exercise:

Exercise: When in Doubt Don't

Think back over a situation where you were uncertain of what to do, rethink what happened.

Could you have waited, and if so would you have had more insight? Do you wish for a "do over", or are you o.k. with your decision. Review and either congratulate yourself on a job well done, or rethink the process so you'll be better prepared for the next time.

As my little piece about doubt points out, judging, doubt and fear go hand in hand, and they take you spiraling away from your center, your peace. This is another pattern that must be broken in order to live a life of fullness. At first, your ego will argue with you. But ask yourself, has the pattern really helped you over the years? Are the same things continuing in your life as they have in the past? If so, why not at least try something new, something different. Start by removing the "emotional charge", the drama.

Drama is the ego's way of keeping you from dealing with the truth of the issue. With unclear thinking it keeps you in the same patterns as before.

Have you heard the expression, "it's not that you shouldn't judge, it's that you can't"?

The reason is, we do not have all the information, ever! Even if we think we do, there is no way for us to know how others feel. We each internalize things according to who we are, what our life experiences have been. After all, it's all about ME! Or at least that is the view of the average person.

At work or in groups we can see the value of having differences, the logistical person needs the conceptual person and vice versa. But let conflict arise and those very things we admired in the other, we will judge. Why is that? Is it because we are attached to a specific outcome...my way or the highway? Are we fearful because we are outside our comfort level? Is it because if you are right, does that mean I am wrong? These are questions that only you can answer and they will be specific to each situation. But to get at the real issue and regain a peaceful environment you must probe to find the answers. What if there is a different outcome, what if I am wrong? What do these mean to You? Does it push your button of control? Do you revert back to childhood issues of what it means to do something wrong/bad?

The "Course in Miracles" says we are never upset for the reason we think we are. The reason for this is because it is not about what was done, but how I feel about it, how I internalize it. Again, it is all about ME!

An example of this might be at the mall when you've been looking for that elusive parking space, you finally find it and while you are waiting for them to back out someone else pulls in from the other direction. At first blush it would appear that you are upset over losing the space, or the rudeness, after all they took YOUR space. But I'd suggest that it's more about your expectation, your personal issues, of being disappointed, being late, etc. We take it personal, and yet more than likely the other driver wasn't even aware we were waiting. After all it's all about THEM!

Misconception is another major factor in judging and realizing that we can't judge. In today's world of electronic communicating there is so much room for misconstruing what is being said. Without the inflection of the tone of voice, the smile on your face, an e-mail or a text can be perceived totally out of context. The other day, while working, Lisa text me and asked if I'd pick up ice cream for a birthday dinner we were having. Because I was hard at work, I quickly shot off a reply of "Y", which in my mind meant "yes". She responded with "cause", it was then I realized what I had done, and text her back. Fortunately Lisa is not one to have her feelings hurt and responded with a LOL, which we did. But this is an example of how easily and quickly things can be misinterpreted, it is always best to give the other person the benefit of the doubt and hope they do the same to you. Try not to be so fast in taking offense. Again, the Golden Rule is a wonderful practice.

Pause a moment in your reading and take the time to do the following exercise:

Exercise: If only I.....

Can you think of a time you were misunderstood, that you took offense when none was meant? Remember and learn from these situations, and allow them to give you pause the next time an opportunity comes up to react.

The unforgiving mind sees itself as innocent and others as guilty. It thrives on conflict and on being right and it sees inner peace as its enemy. It perceives everything as separate....

Gerald Jampolsky

Forgiveness is primarily for our own sake so that we no longer carry the burden of resentment. But to forgive does not mean we allow injustice again....

Jack Kornfield

Judgment always rest in the past, for past experience is the basis on which you judge. Judgment becomes impossible without the past, for without it you do not understand anything....

A Course In Miracles

Judging prevents you from letting go!

Even if the other party is completely wrong, until you have let go of the judgment you will not be at peace. One way to stop judging is to detach from the outcome. Detachment allows everyone their rights and freedom. This is not to say that your personal boundaries might not demand that you leave the situation, the place of turmoil, before you can detach.

Have you ever gone to a football game and had to sit on the "other team's side of the field". Cheering for your team is more difficult and less appreciated than if you were across the field with like minded people.

The definition of "Detachment" includes the follow: Disinterestedness: a lack of bias, prejudice or emotional involvement. In short, the key to detachment is not caring about the outcome, and not caring means that it's not all about you, that you can set aside your issues and see more clearly the other person's view or perhaps their issue, but not buying into it.

Have you ever noticed when it's not your issue/ button how you can be non judgmental; how you can just observe the behavior for what it is? But let there be some of "your stuff" somewhere in there and see how differently you respond.

To the degree you can't let go, that is the same degree or need for you to learn and benefit by the issue that is bothering you. This is the mirror effect of seeing ourselves through others. If it is a small irritant, then maybe all that is needed is to update who you are, to acknowledge this shift in yourself, and then do the "happy dance "that it is so.

You will know you have detached from judgment when there are no emotional hooks when you think of the topic that has bothered you.

In explaining this concept to Jackie, who is one of the most beautiful people I know, both inside and out, I asked her if she would be upset if someone told her "she was an ugly and hateful person". Jackie's response was to laugh and then "why no of course not". Jackie has no issues with her appearance or that she is a kind and caring person. Therefore she has no difficulty whatsoever with detaching from those types of comments. Had she and to the degree she did have that would have been the degree she would have been upset/attached. See how it works?

Pause a moment in your reading and take the time to do the following exercise:

Exercise: The Key to Detachment is that it is not all about you.

Which locks/issues that used to be a concern have you already released?

Which ones are still there?

Just as Judging, Doubt and Fear go hand in hand so does Peace, Forgiveness and Healing.

Which do you choose?

Some unresolved issues we have are like the "Hatfield and McCoys", the feud/patterns have been going on for so long, they just are, they have taken on a life of their own, whether they are relevant now or not.

Remember, this is about breaking patterns. Patterns that do not work for you that you no longer want. I repeat, you are ready or you would not be reading this book. So, unless you enjoy where you are now, what do you have to lose by trying? Set aside your judgment and doubt so that you can take another step toward peace.

Pause a moment in your reading and take the time to do the following exercise:

Exercise: Choose Judgment or Peace

Do you have an event/person in your life that you are at odds with, someone/something that should you come face to face with you would feel anything other than peace? If so, I suggest asking yourself, what is holding you to this place? Why can you not put it to rest? What are your concerns/fears about what it would mean to you to "let go"! Once you have determined what it means to you, you can then be free.

Summary of Chapter Three

- Remove the "emotional charge", the drama. Drama is the ego's way of keeping you from dealing with the truth of the issue with clear thinking. It keeps you in the same old patterns as before.

- Key to detachment is to remember that it is not all about you

- "It's not that you shouldn't judge, it's that you can't".

- Judging another or a situation prevents you from letting go.

- The "Course in Miracles" says we are never upset for the reason we think we are.

- Just as Judging, Doubt and Fear go hand in hand so do Peace, Forgiveness and Healing, which do you choose?

- When in Doubt Don't

Chapter Four

PEACE IS HERE AND NOW

The concept of being in the "Now" is foreign to the Western way of thinking. We pride ourselves on doing just the opposite. We are taught to plan ahead, to be prepared. Now, before I go any further let me say that this does not mean that we don't make plans for our future needs. Everyone has needs that must be addressed prior to the actual time of the need. You cannot wait until you retire to set aside a nest egg, you cannot hope to visit another country or take a vacation of any sort without making arrangements. What I am referring to is while we should be tending to business, seeing to family needs etc. we are obsessing on things down the road, future fears. Most of my fears never materialize and if they do, it is rarely in the manner I envisioned; it's my mind chatter of "what if's,". These bring forward my own personal demons and fears from my past, then project them into my present and future. Remember the Marshmallow Man from the movie Ghostbusters.

Instead, ask yourself is there anything to do now? If so, do it, do not fret, and do not project into the future what you do not want in your life. Once you have done this, leave it alone, until the next time when you need to take action, when something needs to be done on the topic.

One way of knowing that I have done all I need to do at the time is that I have run out of options. That before I can take the next step, I need more input than I have on hand.

By taking things one step at a time, I stay in the NOW which has the side effect of not only peace, but it keeps me from having to retrace my progress, from starting over from the beginning. I can simply go back a few steps to start over and try a different approach, or tactic.

Another way I know if I am too far ahead of myself is that I shut down. Because I have gotten so far in front of me, there are too many options, too many unknown factors to make a decision, my mind has no answers and shuts itself down, or worse continues in the old thought loop, where there is no escape. I shudder when just thinking of this place! It is like the person who walks leading with their head and shoulders. As they get farther away from their center, in this case, over their hips where their weight is centered, they stumble. The same thing happens when we mentally get too far forward of ourselves. Can you think of a time in your life that you have done this, or observed it in someone else?

Being in the "now", allows you to be aware when your peace starts slipping away. There are usually many contributing factors when this occurs, for me lack of sleep, hunger, and not enough quiet time are the things that are guaranteed to start me on a downward spiral. For others it could be sugar, salt, alcohol, caffeine, or a particular hot button to name a few. Watch yourself; keep track of what contributes to your irritable moods, where you are prone to be less than peaceful; you might want to note them on your 30 day calendar you are keeping, in doing so you can stop the downward spiral sooner. This has the benefit of not just allowing you to see how you are contributing to and thus preventing these moments but it shortens the climb back up.

You are making a commitment to yourself, to be a better you, and thereby a better person for everyone in your life. Have you noticed when flying, the flight attendant says, "in the event of an emergency, place the oxygen mask on yourself first, then help others"? The reason for this is clear. Unless we can take care of ourselves we cannot help anyone else.

Pause a moment in your reading and take the time to do the following exercise:

Exercise: Can you name some of the factors that contribute to you getting upset?

Can you see where you are contributing to them and what you can do to change for the better?

In life, as in juggling, success depends on how quickly you are able to let go; one of the things that causes me distress is when it is time to let someone leave my life. It does not matter how the relationship was labeled: friend, spouse, significant other, or just other. There have been times when I have fought against the natural flow and tried to hold onto the relationship long after it needed to be gone.

We are all on a journey; sometimes our paths are parallel with each other and sometimes we part. Years ago, one of my best friends left my life, due to a boundary lesson that we allowed to get out of balance. In doing so neither of us felt good. This type of imbalance is not only unhealthy, but the relationship must "right itself" or "end". Usually both parties feel badly, feel used, which is what happened between my friend and I. While I knew it was necessary it still hurt. I carried the pain and regret with me for a long time. Knowing that it needed to be did not lessen the pain, but it did give me the strength to gradually accept it.

Just recently I saw my friend again, and we had a wonderful moment together. Whether or not anything else comes of this, I feel better that we now have the relationship on a better, higher spiritual footing, I am O.K. with whatever happens. We have all had times when the only way to bring peace to a relationship is to leave it. Just as in my example, the only thing that helps at first is the knowing that it is the right thing to do, that with time you will obtain peace. Sometimes, like in this situation you get a second chance. If this occurs I encourage you not to allow your ego to enter in with defensive, unloving thoughts. Do not miss the opportunity that has been given you. Be in the "Now", do not judge the person or situation based on what occurred in the past, and do not try to recreate it in the NOW, allow the freedom to each of you. In my case, we were not the same people we had been when the rift occurred and because we set aside our past, our relationship benefited.

In life, as in juggling, success depends on how quickly you are able to let go

"In the event of an emergency, place the oxygen mask on yourself first, then help others". The reason for this is clear. Unless we can take care of ourselves we cannot help anyone else.

Furthering the common good does not require that we forgo self interest, but rather that we are able to see our own interest linked to those of others.

Frances Moore Lappe

I used to have a handle on life...but it broke off.

So often, things occur that do not sit well with us, and we take no action. Sometimes we are not even aware of what "it" is or why we don't feel right; just that the little alarm in our solar plexus, our gut, has gone off. There are times when we don't want to make waves; "things are going so well", or we just don't have the energy to confront the issue. Maybe you're not sure that you should be upset, not knowing what the healthy boundary is. This is when the patterns come up and tell us to ignore it, that we have no right to be upset, that it's all in our imagination. It does not matter if the voice is our own or someone else's; the results are still the same, we stuff our feelings and let it ride.

This course of action is all right only if you can let go, if you can forgive and forget. But if there are any feelings of victim/martyr then suppressing them will only bring about problems later, as this energy must and will resurface later. Usually, when it does, it'll be on another topic, one that you feel safe about, and things then get blown out of proportion. This suppressed energy is like a volcano, the longer that it builds the larger the eruption. Unfortunately, the eruption is on something altogether different. There is then the problem that the original issue never gets addressed and will continue to come up, resulting in the same old arguments and disagreements again and again.

Harry went to work for Smith Manufacturing Company working on Charles's team, Harry was always coming up with really innovated ideas that he'd share with Charles. Months later Harry became aware that Charles had taken some of his suggestions up the corporate chain, claiming them as his own. Harry was rightfully upset, but being concerned for his job, after all Charles was his Boss he did not confront him. Unresolved, the resentment grew and grew. Harry no longer spoke up and shared, he was viewed as not a team player, and his snide comments earned him a negative job review, putting his job in jeopardy, the very thing he was trying to avoid. Had Harry taken a different approach of bringing the issue to the forefront, whether with Charles himself or someone else within the company he would have been better off. Perhaps, if he could have let it go, and other new ideas could have been shared in a group, where Harry would have been known as the originator of the suggestion. At is, Charles got the credit and Harry is now seen as a trouble maker, and a negative influence on the team.

Pause a moment in your reading and take the time to do the following exercise:

Exercise: Can you think of a time where you suppressed your strong feelings about something that happened? What were the results? Are you still repeating these patterns? If so, think of a way to handle them differently. Think through what your new responses might be and how they will change the issue.

Be aware when those alarms go off, and know that there are several ways of handling them. If you can discuss it in the moment without the drama and emotion of past patterns, then great, go for it. If it is a highly emotional time, you might want to wait until everyone has calmed down, as angry words generally generate more angry words and resentment. Hopefully, things have not escalated out of control, but if they have, it is much better to have the discussion later, at an agreed upon time or when it is quietly set in your mind. However it is done, it should be addressed within a short time. It is not fair to have it go on; hanging over everyone's head, or you would then become the persecutor.

Do you see how the pattern works, how easily you can continue the roles even when you're trying to improve your skills; how easy it is to change roles, from the victim/martyr to the persecutor?

There are times when it is best to wait, and have no conversation at all, waiting until the moment has passed to make any comment at all. One example of this was taught to me by two men in my life, my business partner and the man I was dating at the time. My business partner had said to me, "Vivian, you are an attractive woman, and have many attractive clothes that look great on you, but the other day, that outfit you had on really was not flattering." I agreed with him and that evening told my date what had been said. My date asked if I was angry about the comment. When I said no, he responded by saying that if *he* had made the comment I would have been angry. This was a true statement, and it puzzled me. What was the difference? Then it occurred to me, my business partner waited to tell me several days later when I had something else on. He waited until I was no longer "in the energy " of what needed to be said. Had he made his comment that day, I would have felt bad, and my ego's need to defend myself might have risen.

So, you see, sometimes by waiting until we no longer own or are attached to our actions things can be said and appreciated without the negative emotional feelings that might otherwise come about. I cannot emphasize enough, that it is not necessary to get this "right" the first few times. Give yourself permission not to be perfect. The ego would have you blame yourself and then give up on the idea that you can make progress. Sometimes the hardest thing to do is the thing that needs be done the most. If you experience difficulty, then great, you are on the right path. Just keep on, keep trying and adjusting until you find your way; it will be worth it I promise.

So many times, we do not even know what the right way is, or what the problem to address is. This is where the mirror concept comes in so handy. Simply put, we do not see ourselves, however it is easy to see what others are doing wrong in their lives, and so we are given people that mirror us. Sometimes it is the exact issue, a portion of it, or the exact opposite. An example of this would be someone that gives too much, so they are drawn to people who are selfish. This is the extreme of the same lesson, personal boundaries.

Give yourself permission not to be perfect.

A diamond is a piece of coal that stuck to the job.

Michael Larson

It is easier to be wise for others than for yourself.

LaRouchefoucauld

Withdraw into yourself and look. And if you do not find yourself beautiful as yet, do as the creator of a statue that is to be made beautiful; he cuts away here, he smoothes there, he makes this line lighter, this other purer, until he has shown a beautiful face upon the statue...

Potinus

All of nature knows the need for boundaries. Growing up we had an old yellow tomcat, that we cleverly called "Kitty". Kitty had no problem with boundaries, his yard was his! When a dog came into his yard there would be a fight, with all the usual noise and aftermath. Win or lose, he always stood his ground. Another boundary Kitty had was with children; a small child could do things that would earn an older child a scratch. I am not sure how he knew when we should have known better but he did, and just as with the dogs, he enforced his boundaries without fail. I have a rule of thumb, that if it is not right for one, then it is not right for the other people involved. The universe does not believe in the victim/martyr system.

Once you notice a situation or pattern in someone else that you are bothered with, look to your life for the mirroring issues. Remember it really is never about the other person, everything is a reflection of us, of our life's lessons.

Pause a moment in your reading and take the time to do the following exercise:

Exercise: Look into your Mirror

Think of a situation that really bothers you, can you see an aspect of yourself in it?

Can you determine the real reason you are upset?

Summary of Chapter Four

- Most fears never materialize and if they do, it is rarely in the manner we envisioned.

- Ask yourself is there anything to do Now? If so do it.

- The power is in the Now, in each and every moment. For this is the only time in which you can take action.

- One way of knowing that I have done all I need to do at the time is that I have run out of options. That before I can take the next step, I need more input than I have on hand.

- Another way of knowing you have ventured from your "Now" is that you mentally shut down. Having too many options, and too many unknown factors to make a decision, the mind has no answers and shuts itself down, or worse continues in the old thought loop, where there is no escape.

- Can you name some of the factors that contribute to you getting upset?

- Can you see how you are contributing to them and what you can do to change for the better?

- This suppressed energy is like a volcano, the longer that it builds the larger the eruption. Usually, the eruption is on something altogether different, and the original issue never gets addressed and will continue to come up, resulting in the same old arguments and disagreements again and again. Can you think of a situation where you have done this? What were the results?

- Angry words generally generate more angry words and resentment, and it is better to never have made the comment than to apologize for it later.

- We are given people that mirror us. Sometimes it is the exact issue, a portion of it, or the exact opposite; after all it is easier to see others than ourselves. Think of a situation that really bothers you, can you see as aspect of yourself in it? Can you determine the real reason you are upset?

Chapter Five

THE LAST WORD

All too often we point out the negative in ourselves and others. I want you to be equally aware of the positive. Focus on that which you want. Keep your eyes on your goal, what you hope to accomplish, and the life you want to live. Twice a day, as you wake and go to sleep review your goals. Daydream of what you want to achieve, visualize them. See them happening, make them real. Include this in your 30 day calendar. Any goal worth having is worth working for so stay the course, and be gentle with yourself.

In writing this book, I wanted to have a deadline for completion. What I had to come to terms with is that the book was but another part of my personal growth and it was only as I learned and processed my lessons that the book proceeded. There are many days I simply could not write, as peace was not something within me, certainly nothing that I could write about. There is an expression that says that you learn what you are teaching, and then I'd understand why I needed to get back to writing. I am no different from anyone else. I like to think, "No really, I've already worked through that, and it is not an issue for me any longer. But issues are like onions; there are many kinds and they have many layers to them that must be peeled away, one at a time until you reach the center, and it is no bigger than a scallion.

But issues are like onions; they have many layers to them that must be peeled away, one at a time until you reach the center, and it is no bigger than a scallion.

Don't try to push the river. There is a natural flow to everything, the more you learn to live in sync with your world, the more peaceful, productive, and joyful you become. I am not advocating giving up when things become difficult; as you see the book was written, but in its own time, not by my deadline.

Should you have to look at the same issue over and over, this should not be seen as a failure, but rather a natural part of the process. The key is to see the differences in what and how you respond each time. Acknowledge the changes that you have made, the progress, knowing that another layer of the onion has been peeled away. Do not be discouraged, thus allowing your ego to tell you things are not changing, because they are. They must. Just keep up the good work and keep your obtainable goal of inner peace in mind. As all beach lovers know, when caught in a rip tide, you are told not to fight the current. Rather swim parallel with the shore, your goal, until the resistance weakens and you can then swim in. In short go with the flow, keeping your goal in sight until it is reachable. You and your world will be a better place for it. So remember stay focused, stay positive and know that with each try you are a step closer. After all a blizzard starts with just one snowflake at a time.

It's your choice, so remember to choose peace and joy.